Children's Music Worksh

presents

Christmas Jazz Piano Sheet Music

Easy to Play Jazz Arrangements of Classic Traditional Christmas songs With online mp3 audio recordings

www.musicfunbooks.com/xmas

Children's Music Workshop • P.O. Box 1247, Pacific Palisades, CA 90272

Christmas Jazz Song List

Angels From The Realms Of Glory

Traditional

Medium fast

MP3 audio recordings availabe at www.musicfunbooks.com/xmas

Angels We Have Heard On High

Medium

Auld Lang Syne

Ballad

Away in a Manger #1

Slow

MP3 audio recordings availabe at www.musicfunbooks.com/xmas

Away in a Manger #2

Medium

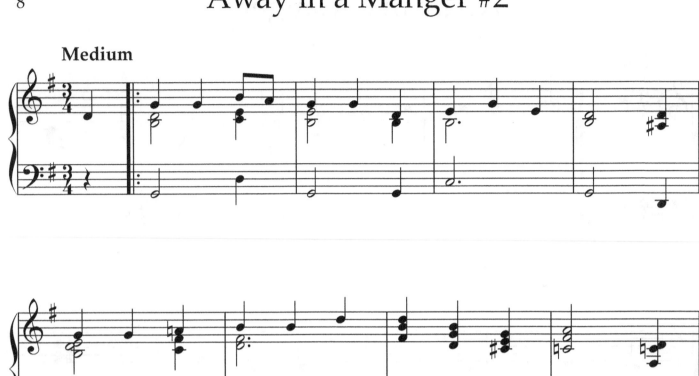

MP3 audio recordings availabe at www.musicfunbooks.com/xmas

The Boar's Head Carol

Medium

Bring a Torch, Jeanette, Isabella

Flowing

Carol of the Bells

Medium

MP3 audio recordings availabe at www.musicfunbooks.com/xmas

Christmas Was Born On Christmas Day

Medium

Coventry Carol

Medium slow

The First Noel

Medium slow

The Friendly Beasts

From Heaven Above To Earth I Come

Fum, Fum, Fum

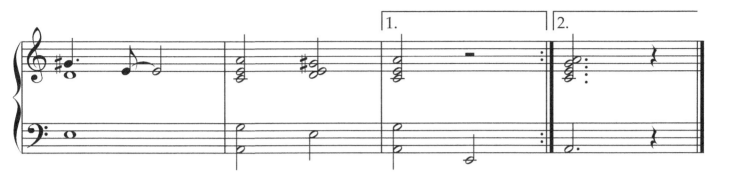

Jazz Waltz

Gesu Bambino

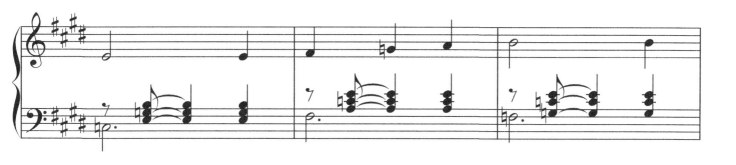

Go, Tell It On The Mountain

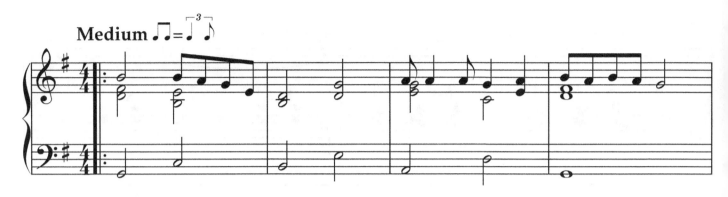

MP3 audio recordings availabe at www.musicfunbooks.com/xmas

God Rest Ye Merry, Gentlemen

Medium slow

MP3 audio recordings availabe at www.musicfunbooks.com/xmas

Good Christian Men, Rejoice

Medium

MP3 audio recordings availabe at www.musicfunbooks.com/xmas

Good King Wenceslas

Medium fast

Hark! The Herald Angels Sing

Medium

Here We Come A-wassailing

Medium fast

The Holly And The Ivy

It Came Upon The Midnight Clear

Medium

Jingle Bells

MP3 audio recordings availabe at www.musicfunbooks.com/xmas

Joy To The World

Medium fast

Noel! Noel!

O Christmas Tree

Medium

MP3 audio recordings availabe at www.musicfunbooks.com/xmas

O Come, All Ye Faithful

Medium

MP3 audio recordings availabe at www.musicfunbooks.com/xmas

O Come, O Come Emmanuel

Slow

MP3 audio recordings availabe at www.musicfunbooks.com/xmas

O Holy Night

Medium

MP3 audio recordings availabe at www.musicfunbooks.com/xmas

O Little Town Of Bethlehem

Ballad

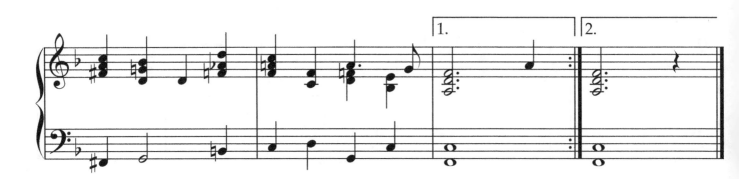

MP3 audio recordings availabe at www.musicfunbooks.com/xmas

Silent Night

Slow

MP3 audio recordings availabe at www.musicfunbooks.com/xmas

Sing We Now Of Christmas

Medium

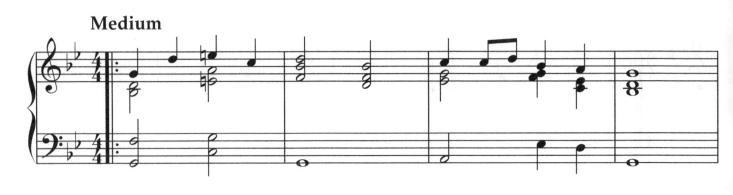

MP3 audio recordings availabe at www.musicfunbooks.com/xmas

Still, Still, Still

Medium

Toyland

Medium slow

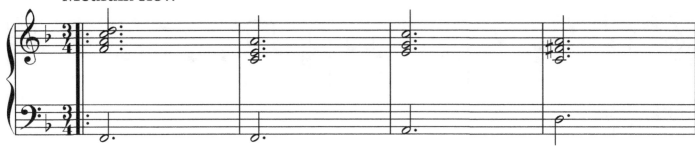

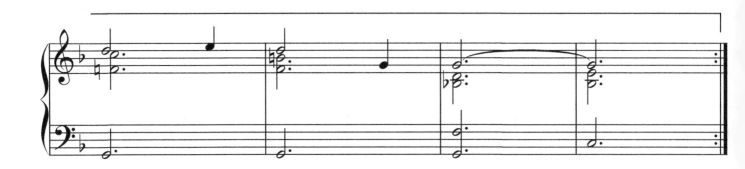

Twelve Days Of Christmas

Medium

MP3 audio recordings availabe at www.musicfunbooks.com/xmas

Up On The Housetop

Medium fast

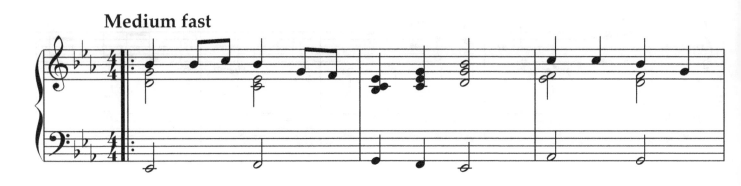

We Three Kings Of Orient Are

Medium

MP3 audio recordings availabe at www.musicfunbooks.com/xmas

We Wish You A Merry Christmas

Bright

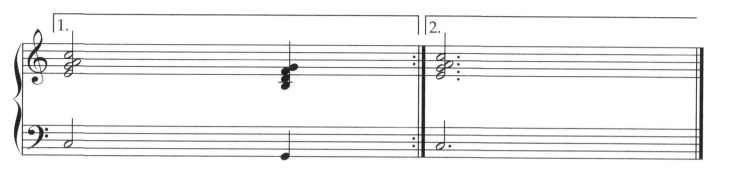

What Child is This?

Medium

MP3 audio recordings availabe at www.musicfunbooks.com/xmas

While Shepherds Watched Their Flocks

Medium

Made in the USA
Las Vegas, NV
08 November 2024

11347075R00037